CONTENTS

1.

The well-known Terra-cotta Museum is located east of Emperor Qin's Mausoleum, which covers a total area of 20 hectares. The museum is decorated with verdant trees, blooming flowers and carpets of green grass. The scenery in the museum looks quite elegant and delightful. Three main buildingsof the museum, which were named Pit 1, Pit 2 and Pit 3, were constructed on their original sites in different periods of time.

It was on March 29,1974,when local farmers of XiYang Village, LingTong County, were drilling a series of wells in search of water, some pottery fragments and ancient bronze weapons were discovered accidentally. The head of the village reported the news to the local government at once. The news aroused much attention from both local government and National Cultural Relics Bureau. With government approval, an archaeological team from Shaanxi Province arrived at the site on July 17, 1974 and began their explorations and excavations. On October 1st, 1979, Emperor QinShihuang's Terra-cotta Museum was opened to the public. By the time

of the opening ceremony, archaeologists have excavated the area of 2,000 square meters in Pit 1 and some 1,087 terra-cotta warriors and horses were displayed there after restoration. The village which used to be never known by outside, usually quiet, became restless since then. The archaeological wonder discovered here came as a shock to the country as well as to the whole world. Following the discovery of Pit 1, Pit 2 and Pit 3 were brought to light in April and May of 1976. Pit 3 was opened in 1989. Pit 2 started to be excavated in March 1994 and was opened in October the same year while it was being excavated. Besides three pits, two sets of bronze chariots and horses discovered in the west of Emperor Qin's Mausoleum in December in 1980, were on display in the museum after restoration.

In the last 20 years, the Terra-cotta Museum has developed and become the largest on-site museum in China. The museum staff has increased. More and more valuable cultural relics have been unearthed successively. The archae-

ological research is fruitful. Pit 1 is a huge arch-domed steel structure, located at the center of the museum with an area of 16,000 square meters. The other two pits were built in Qin and Han Dynasty's tomb mound style, covering an area of 17, 934 and 1, 694 square meters respectively. The multiple exhibition halls lies to the east of Pit 2, covering an area of 7,100 square meters, provides a series of exhibits, such as two sets of bronze chariots and horses, the new findings from the Emperor Qin's Mausoleum, the history of the Museum and all kinds of temporary exhibits. These displays systematically depict the history of the Qin Dynasty from 221BC-206BC and can help the viewers to have a better understanding on the Terra-cotta Warriors and Horses. The south of Pit 1 is a circle vision hall. The movie inside lasts 20 minutes and provides vivid materials for telling the story of Emperor Qin and his Terra-cotta Army 2,200 years ago. The halls on the northwest of Pit 3, which covers 4,282 square meters,are the

multiple service halls where the visitors can have meal, do shopping and take a rest.

Emperor Qin's Terra-cotta Museum is not only a treasure house where the tourists can learn history, culture and human civilization, but also a main scenic spot of Xi'an city. It can receive about 1.5 million tourists annually. Approximately 40 million visitors from home and abroad have visited the Museum within the last 20 years. Today " the Eighth Wonder of the world" has almost become synonym of the Terra-cotta Warriors and Horses. In 1987, the Emperor Qin's Mausoleum was put on the list of the UNESCO as a world-class cultural heritage site. Now the Museum is well-known widely as a huge modern on-site museum and it is going to be one of the best in the world.

The multiple service halls ◆ • • • • • • • •

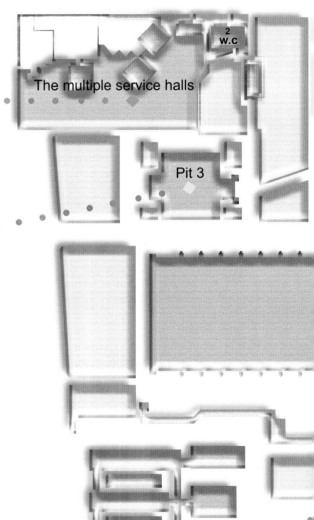

The multiple service halls

2
W.C

Pit 3

Pit 3

The circle vision hall

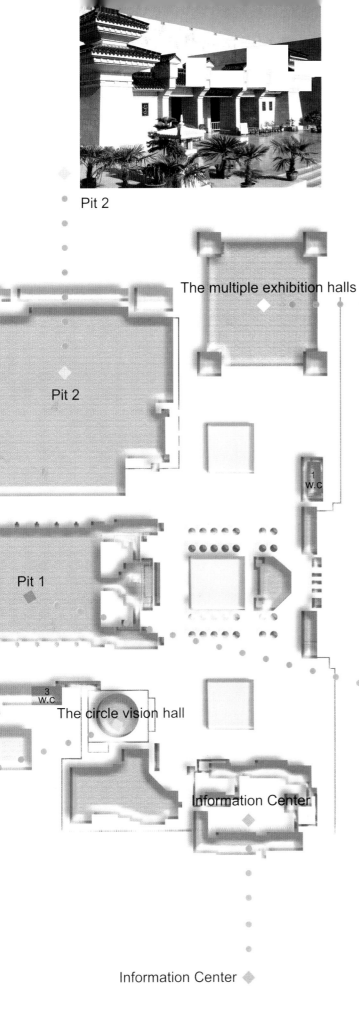
Pit 2

N

The multiple exhibition halls

Pit 2

The multiple exhibition halls

1
w.c

3
w.c
The circle vision hall

Pit 1

Information Center

Information Center ◆

Pit 1

Awakened
Qin's Terra-Cotta Army

Many important men have crossed the Chinese historical stage during the last 5,000 years. One of the most important was to be known later as Emperor QinShihuang, the first emperor in Chinese history. Born the son of King ZhuangXiang, the King of Qin, in the first month of the lunar year in 259 BC, he was first named ZhaoZheng and later his name was changed to YingZheng. YingZheng's mother was a beautiful concubine of LuBuwei, the merchant who the king had met while he was hostage in the nearby State of Zhao, prior to ascending the throne. In 247 BC, when YingZheng was only 13 years old, his father died and he ascended the throne as the King of Qin. Being too young to handle the affairs of the State, LuBuwei served as his regent and the Prime Minister, together with YingZheng's mother, the Queen, administered the State of Qin. At the age of 22, Ying-Zheng took over the reigns of the government himself. The first decision that he made was to put down a rebellion, which was led by LaoAi, a servant who had become intimate with the Queen. The following year, the young king removed his former regent, LuBuwei and exiled him to SiChuan where he later committed suicide. Having all of his own civil affairs in order, the king began the task of conquering the six other states. Beginning in 230 BC, the King of Qin waged many battles against the states of Qi, Chu, Yan, Han, Zhao and Wei. Finally, in 221 BC, the King of Qin achieved his final victory and unified the Qin Empire. His territory extended from the sea in the south and east, LinTao in the west and finally to Mount Yin and the area of LiaoDong in the north. It was at this time, at the age of 39 that the King of Qin declared himself to be "QinShiHuangDi", the first emperor of the Qin. Feudal separation that had lasted since the Spring and Autumn Periods had finally come to an end. In order to consolidate his rule, Emperor Qin instituted a series of new policies. Probably his greatest contribution to the practice of government in China was his establishment of the centralized State and abolition of the feudal system. He divided the country into 36 prefectures that were further broken down into counties, townships, "Tings" and "Lis". He appointed twelve ministers who helped him make decisions on state affairs. By appointing the ministers directly, Emperor Qin had all the powers of the State in his hands.

Qinshihuang - the first emperor of China and the founder of the Qin Dynasty

To further unify the country, Emperor Qin standardized the system of weights and measures, handwriting into Small Seal Script and then went on to regulate the width of carriage axles to six feet. All these measures helped to establish a high centralization of politics, economy, military affairs and culture. In a further attempt to control and protect his ideological policies, Emperor Qin destroyed many ancient records and burned Confucian writings. He once ordered over 400 Confucian scholars to be killed by the Wei River and another 700 scholars buried alive at the foot of Mount Li.

In order to have the social situation under control, he spent a lot of time on reading reports from all parts of the country. He even had the documents weighed (Writings were inscribed on bamboo or wood at that time) every morning and night, and would not rest till a certain weight had passed through his hands.

Ensuring the security of his new empire was a major concern of Emperor Qin. An imperial road network on an unprecedented scale was ordered to

A view of the Great Wall

erected wherever he went for leaving Emperor's merits and virtues, ordering his people to abide by the law of the State of Qin. Undoubtedly the First Emperor's greatest and most impressive achievement in this respect was his connecting and rebuilding of the defensive walls previously built by different states in the Warring States Period. He appointed General MengTian as commander-in-chief of the Imperial forces who had already distinguished himself in subduing the Xiong-nu Tartars in the far north and northwest, with the task of building the wall. Thus came into the Great Wall of China, one of the wonders in the world. A huge labor force was organized to complete this construction. Moreover, Emperor Qin sent his army to guard five mountains in southern part of China and ordered the Lin Canal to construct. All these measures played such an active role in establishing a unified country - Qin State.

On the evidence of history, QinShihuang was not only well known as an outstanding man but also was extremely cruel and arbitrary. After he won the empire, the construction of his tomb was intensified and a massive palace building program was

build and a highway was opened straight through Capital XianYang to the northern border. He used to have his five tours of inspection on such an imperial route to far- flung corners of his domain. Stone memorial tablets with inscriptions were

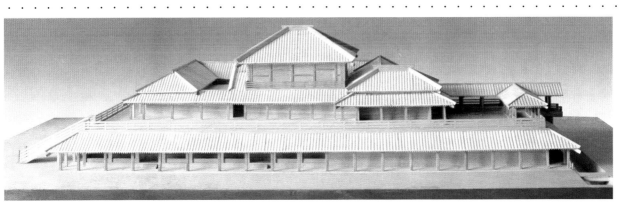

Drawing of the Qin Imperial Palace at Capital XianYang

embarked. For example the Apang Palace at Capital XianYang was built with "terraces that could seat ten thousand". SiMaqian's (145BC-86BC) ShiJi (Records of Historians) records: "Three hundred palaces were built within the Pass, and east of it more than four hundred. A large labor force was drafted to build Apang Palace and the emperor's tomb." The population of the State of Qin was around twenty million then, but all kinds of labors for construction were two million, making up one tenth of the total population. The social economic development was seriously restricted by the truth that a large labor force left their farms for these luxurious buildings. The costs in men and material began to threaten the Empire's economy.

Having been impressed by certain magical notions, QinShihuang employed great energies and resources in his search for the elixir of immortality, beginning in earnest in 219 BC. He was told "in the middle of the sea, there are three supernatural mountains called PengLai, FongZhang and Ying Zhou. Immortals live there". He was even told to go there together with several thousand young boys and girls, out to sea to search the Immortals. These attempts continued but without success. Instead the overwork in seeking for the Immortal caused Emperor's earlier death at the age of 50.

Because QinShihuang was obsessed with a fear of death in his whole life, no ministers dared to mention the word "death" before him while he was

seriously sick on his last inspection tour through the Empire. But the truth was that Emperor's illness got worse and worse. At this moment he nominated his eldest son FuSu who was full of political ability to succeed to the throne and the letter confirming that succession had been entrusted to ZhaoGao, keeper of Chariots, for safe keeping and eventual delivery. Emperor hoped that this letter would let FuSu come back to the capital XianYang immediately and hold his funeral after his death. But ZhaoGao delayed the Imperial letter till QinShihuang died in ShaQiu, present JuLu County, HeBei Province in 210 BC.

As Emperor Qin died away from the capital, the Prime Minister LiSi hushed the matter up for fear that there would be troubles among the contending princes in XianYang. So there were only few people who knew the truth. LiSi, ZhaoGao had other ideas on the succession and wished to appoint another son, HuHai, whom ZhaoGao had taught writing and could influence and control easily. Thus Zhao and Li conspired to destroy the Imperial letter and forge a decree appointing HuHai as Crown Prince. At the same time, the eldest son FuSu and commander-in-chief MengTian were ordered to commit suicide. While waiting for news of suicide, they made a detour purposely back to XianYang.

Because of the long journey and hot weather in July, the corpse of Emperor was decomposing. In order to cover up the smell, they had one chariot fully loaded with abalone fish following Emperor's chariot. When they were approaching to XianYang, the news of suicide from FuSu and MengTian arrived and then the obituary was released. In September of that year, the dead body of Emperor Qin was buried inside his mausoleum.

Later that same year HuHai succeeded to the throne, becoming the Second Emperor of Qin. HuHai was such a man lacking political ability and being spoiled too much since he was young. He could hardly make any final decision on court affairs, so power gradually fell into ZhaoGao's hands. In spite of his comparative youth on court affairs, the Second Emperor sought to emulate his father on a life of luxury. What he did went even farther than Emperor QinShihuang. In 209 BC, a peasant rebellion on a large scale in Chinese history ended the Qin Empire. The Qin Empire only lasted for fifteen years from 221 BC to 206 BC, but its development in various fields laid a foundation for and exerted far-reaching influence on the development of various dynasties in Chinese history thereafter.

3.

Emperor Qin's Mausoleum is situated at the northern foot of Mount Li, some 35 kilometers east of Xi'an city. Mount Li stands 1,256 meters high with trees evergreen all year around. The ShuiJingZhu (The Water Classic) records: "The southern side of Mount Li is famous for gold and the northern side jade." The main reason why the emperor selected this site as his mausoleum is due to its good FengShui.

FengShui is the art and science of positioning man-made structures in harmony with the vital cosmic energy coursing through the earth. It is quite essentially for Chinese in its concern for harmony and proportion, and for balancing man, nature and spirit.

Traditional cosmology describes how the invisible energy currents, or "Dragon Veins", run from the sky down into mountain peaks and then along the earth, blending heavenly and earthly energies. Natural topography-the forms of hills, the direction of streams-is believed to modify the natural energies, creating auspicious and inauspicious sites.

The ideal site faces south, with rising land to the east and softly undulating hills to the west. It has a stream in the front and mountains in the back and is open to breezes in front, is dry and has no white ants. Often these sites are used for graves: ancestors must be appeased with the best of everything.

According to FengShui theory, Emperor Qin's Mausoleum was finally decided to construct on the site with evergreen Mount Li to the south and the Wei River to the north. Another reason for the emperor to select his mausoleum here was that this site was also the burial area of the Qin Kings. Since the capital of the State of Qin moved from west to east of China, the political center changed and the burials of the Qin Kings moved, too. Ancient Chinese paid a lot of attention on burying their tribes men nearby the capital. After the capital was founded in XianYang, the zone between XianYang and Mount Li became the burial region for the Qin family. The tomb of emperor Qin's father is only about 10 kilometers west of him.

The massive construction of Emperor Qin's Mausoleum created a precedent for the emperors after him. Burial mounds that conceal tombs below appeared early in the late Spring and Autumn Period (770 BC-476 BC), but none of them had been as huge as Emperor QinShihuang's Mausoleum. So the custom of building a huge Mausoleum started from Emperor Qin and the emperors in the later dynasties like Han, Tang etc. began to follow. The Emperor Qin's Mausoleum was originally named LiShan Garden. In ancient times, people did not worship their gods and ancestors at the graves and tombs. But it was since QinShihuang who had his resting hall built by the side of mausoleum. LiYi, covering an area of 7.5 square kilometers, which was the administrative office of the tomb, was set up in the vicinity of the mausoleum. This was also the first in Chinese history.

The mausoleum started to be under construction soon after QinShihuang became King of Qin. The men in charge of construction were the Ministers of Qin Empire then, such as LuBuwei, Lisi and so on. But ShaoFu, an apparatus of the Central Government, took charge of it particularly. It is estimated that construction took 38 years from 247 BC to 208 BC and it could be divided into three phases: At the beginning, the construction was on small scale, this was the first phase from 247 BC to 230 BC. The project was intensified from 230 BC to 221 BC. This was the second phase. It was during these ten years that the State of Qin won the battles successively to annex the other six states for unifying the country. The State of Qin was strong enough to provide considerable material resources and manpower for the mausoleum's building. Though the scale during this period was larger than in previous periods, it was smaller than the one in the next period, because the State of Qin still paid more attention on the unified wars. The third phase was from 221 BC to 208 BC, the construction came into its peak times. There were at most 720,000 conscripts worked there.

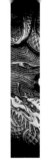

The burial mound of QinShihuang's tomb, situated 1.5 kilometers west of the Terra-cotta Museum

The construction of Emperor Qin's Mausoleum lasted near 40 years. Thousands of thousands of people were involved in this huge construction. When the tomb was too deep to dig in, a report arrived from Minister LiSi: " It seemed that we had reached the bottom of the earth and could not dig in any more". Even then Emperor ordered to try again. It is apparent that the emperor took care a lot of his mausoleum and required it as big as possible.

Emperor Qi died in 210 BC while on his fifth travel through the empire. He was devoted to his constant search for the elixir of immortality in whole life. He could not believe he was going to leave this world at the age of only 50. When his dead body was buried in the tomb, the entire construction of the mausoleum was not completed. According to a decree of the Second Emperor, those of his father's ladies who had no children were ordered to follow the emperor to the grave, as well as a lot of tomb builders buried alive. Emperor Qin's funeral was described by HanShu(Book of Han) as follows: " thousands of officials were killed and thousands of craftsmen were buried alive with the purpose of keeping secret." The construction was roughly finished during the reign of the Second Emperor because a series of the peasant's revolts happened.

Emperor Qin believed that the life under the ground was a continuation of it in the world, he ordered such a huge mausoleum to be constructed 2,200 years ago. At the same time he left his highly developed civilization to people today.

Awakened
Qin's Terra-Cotta Army

4.

Emperor Qin's Mausoleum and The Satellite Pits and Tombs

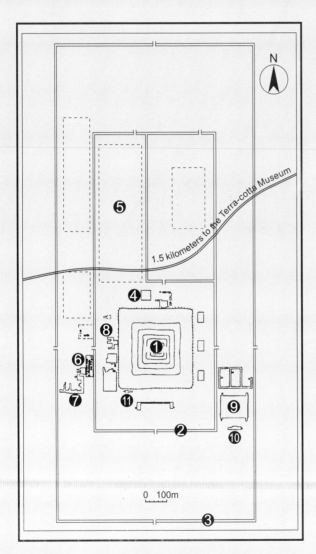

Location map showing Emperor Qin's Mausoleum and some discovered satellite pits and tombs

1. The burial mound of QinShihuang's tomb
2. Inner wall of burial mound
3. Outer wall of burial mound
4. The resting hall
5. The side hall
6. Pits of rare birds and animals
7. Stable Pits
8. Pit of two sets of bronze chariots and horses
9. Pit of stone armor and helmets
10. Pit of terra-cotta acrobats
11. Pit of terra-cotta civil officials

Emperor QinShihuang's Mausoleum looks huge and magnificent and can be seen from afar. The construction of the emperor's tomb is recorded in the ShiJi(Records of the historian) as follows: they dug through three subterranean streams and poured molten copper for the outer coffin, and the tomb was fitted with models of palaces, pavilions and officials, as well as fine vessels, precious stones and rarities. Artisans were ordered to fix up crossbows so that any thief breaking in would be shot. All the country's streams, the Yellow River and Yangtze were reproduced in quicksilver and by some mechanical means made to flow. The heavenly constellations were shown above and the regions of the earth below. The candles were made of whale oil to ensure their burning for eternity." The description can provide us that Emperor QinShihuang's tomb was actually an undergrund treasure-house. The tomb was a subterranean palace with a protective outer wall 6,210 meters in perimeter on the ground level. Within this area was an inner wall that surrounded the burial mound, located in the southern half of overall compound. Both of the walls had gates leading out in all four directions and watch towers. The burial mound was 115 meters high 2,200 years ago, it's reduced to a height of 76 meters today due to the passage of time. With the emperor's tomb as the center, some 600 satellite pits and tombs have been found around within the area of 56.25 square kilometers. Since the discovery of the pits of the Terra-cotta Warriors and Horses in 1974, more and more satellite pits and tombs began to be known and unearthed.

The bronze music bell with gold-silver-inlaid patterns

The resting hall of the emperor is situated 5 meters north of the burial mound. It was once a large building above the ground covering an area of 3,575 square meters, where there were all the necessities for daily life, as if the emperor were still alive. The side hall, a subsidiary building of the resting hall, is located north of the resting hall, in which the tomb owner could rest and relax.

Three sets of ruins, probably small palaces of some sort have been discovered in the northwest corner between the inner wall and the outer wall. They were most likely ritual sites and living quarters for the tomb officials, because some pieces of relics unearthed from here such as a bronze music bell with gold-silver-inlaid inscription, a bronze Quan, the standard weighing apparatus, fragments of a bronze lamp with goose-shaped leg, some broken pieces of a porcelain bottle and tiles etc. can reveal.

The half-round eaves tile which measures 48cm in height and 61cm in diameter is the largest ancient tile thus discovered from the ruin of the resting hall.

Full view of the excavation site of the stable pit

1 Pits of Rare Birds and Animals:

Thirty-one pits of rare animals and birds with a few attendants to the west of the mausoleum have been unearthed within the confines of the wall. These finds indicated Emperor's love for hunting, everything known to him was buried with him after his death.

2 Stable Pits:

Ninety-eight sets of the stable pits at ShangJiaoCun, a village 350 meters east of the mausoleum, were found. In front of the horses were placed some pottery jars, basins and lamps in these pits. The remains of millets and hay were still left in the basins. These pits were modeled after Qin's imperial stable system and of certain significance in the history of the horse-raising method.

The pottery figures of the kneeling attendants excavated in the stable pit

The iron lamp

The pottery plate

The pottery lamp

The pottery jar

The pottery basin

3 Tombs of Emperor Qin's Children:

Archaeologists have found seventeen Qin tombs for Emperor QinShihuang's princes and princesses killed by the Second Emperor. They were placed eight meters on both sides of the stable pits. While eight of these tombs have been unearthed, they are in 甲-shape with sloping roadways leading to the tombs. Approximately two hundred historical relics made of different materials, such as gold, silver, bronze, iron, pottery, jade, shellfish, bone, etc. have been discovered, and lacquer wares, fragmented silk fabrics, too.

4 Mass Graves:

In present day ZhaoBeiHuCun, a village to the southwest of the mausoleum, there have been discovered "mass graves", covering an area of 8,100 square meters. 42 of them have been unearthed already and over a hundred human skeletons were found. The excavations show that the skeletons were roughly put together in the simple graves, and one such grave with the skeletons overlapped, some of them are in struggling position, it means that they were buried alive. On the evidence of inscription with the names and birth places of the death on tile fragments, the earliest epitaphs which have been unearthed so far, it is presumably that these were the laborers who died during the construction work.

The tile fragments with inscriptions of the names and birth places of the death, the earliest epitaphs which have been unearthed so far

Full view of the excavation site of the Bronze Chariots and Horses

The restored No.1 Chariot--High Chariot

The restored No.2 Chariot-Comfortable Chariot

5 Pit of Two Sets of Bronze Chariots and Horses:

In December 1980, archaeologists discovered a large pit holding two sets of painted bronze chariots and horses, 20 meters west of the Emperor Qin's tomb mound. The pit is about 7.8 meters beneath the present ground level with the bronze chariots and horses placed in a big wood coffin originally. Due to the passage of time, wood had rotted and the covering earthen layers had collapsed. When excavated, the chariots and horses were damaged into thousands of pieces. Fortunately, the pit had not been stolen, all the broken pieces were overlapped in disorder on the ground. Through eight years' painstaking restoration by the archaeologists, the complete two sets of bronze chariots and horses are now on display in the museum.

Investigation reveals that the chariots were the deluxe sedans used by the emperor when he went on inspection tours in his after life. They were exactly modeled after the real chariot, horse and driver, but made in half size. Bronze was used for making chariots, horses and charioteers and large amount of gold

and silver used as ornament. Both chariots and horses were cast in perfect proportion. The exquisite color paintings made the bronze chariots look more magnificent and noble. As a result of study and research, archaeologists named them "High Chariot" and "Comfortable Chariot" respectively. Each chariot had a single shaft, two wheels and was drawn by four horses. These are the biggest, most deluxe, structurally most realistic and best preserving bronze chariots and horses that have been unearthed so far.

High Chariot: The chariot with the horses in the front is totally 2.57 meters long and weighs about 1,061 kilos. It is regarded as "Battle Carriage" or "Inspection Carriage", too. On the outer side of the left protecting board there is an arrow quiver in which 12 bronze arrows are laid. While on the inner right side of the protective board there is a bronze shield inserted in a set of silver shield-holder. Both sides of the shield are colorfully painted by cloud-like patterns. This shield is the most intact and complete one ever discovered from the Qin Dynasty.

To restore No.1 Chariot

The charioteer stands on the chariot is looking ahead with prudent and humble facial expression. He is wearing the headgear and his square-toed shoes curve slightly towards the ankles. He is armed with a long sword and decorated with a jade ring at the waist. Both of his hands are extending forward. The thumb is apart from the forefinger, while the other three fingers are together holding bridle reins. The fingers are thin and long, the fingernails are round and full. The vivid imitation made two hands look like real ones.

Comfortable Chariot: It is about 3.17 meters together with the horses and weighs about 1,241 kilos. The carriage is longer and divided into a front chamber and a back chamber. The front chamber is for a sitting charioteer riding the carriage. The costumes of the High Chariot's driver and the Comfortable Chariot's driver are the same, but the sitting driver looks more humble. The back chamber is quite spacious, 0.78 meters wide and 0.88 meters long. The window panels of the back chamber are cast into shallow diamond-flower holes, which are neatly aligned into rhombic patterns. The holes are used for ventilation. So the Comfortable Chariot is also named "Air-conditioned Carriage" 2,200 years ago.

The roof of the carriage is a turtle-shell canopy. The canopy is 1.78 meters long, 1.29 meters wide.

Workmanship: The thinness of bronze cast walls is one of the significant characteristics of the bronze chariots. The thickest position of the canopies of two chariots is 4mm,whereas the thinnest place only 2mm. The canopy of the Comfortable Chariot covers an area of 2.3 square meters. This is not an easy job to accomplish even today.

Restoration of the canopy of No.1Chariot

Restoration of the canopy of No.1Chariot

The restored canopy of No.1 Chariot

Charioteer of No.2 Chariot

Charioteer of No.1 Chariot

Charioteer of No.1 Chariot with reins in hands

Charioteer of No.2 Chariot with reins in hands

Back view of the Charioteer of No.1 Chariot

Jade ring at the waist for decoration

Back view of the horses

The arrow quiver in the carriage of No.1 Chariot

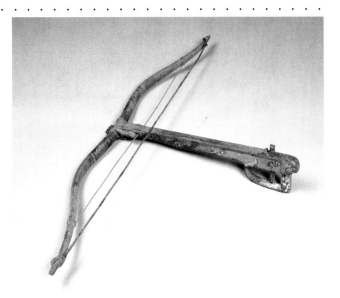

The crossbow in No.1 Chariot

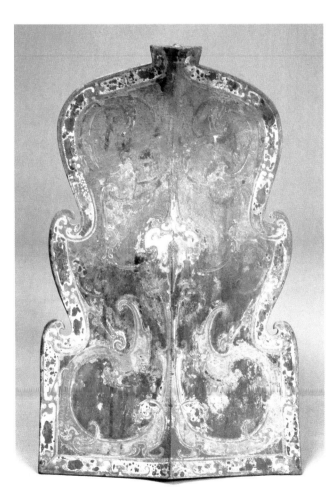

Color painting on the front surface of the shield

Color painting on the inside surface of the shield

Driving and Harnessing Mechanism: Both High Chariot and Comfortable Chariot are of the single-shaft type. The driving process is "horses puling the yokes, yokes are linked with the balance block, balance block pulling the shaft, and the shaft pulling the carriage". Each chariot has four horses, two central-horses and two side horses. In order to keep the four horses pull steady and the chariots walk smoothly, there is each a bronze belly-drive suspended at the outer ribs of the two central-horses. On the end of the belly-drive are cast with four sharp cones protruding toward the side horses. In case the side horse walks in, the four sharp cones would stab and pain it. If the side horse walks out, the rope round the side horse would be stretched tight.

From the teeth engraved in the mouths of the horses, it is evident that the eight horses to the chariots are all six years old, at the best age for draught. The coarse-fiber tassel on the head of each right side horse is the symbol of the social position and authority.

Belly-drive between the central-horse and the side-horse

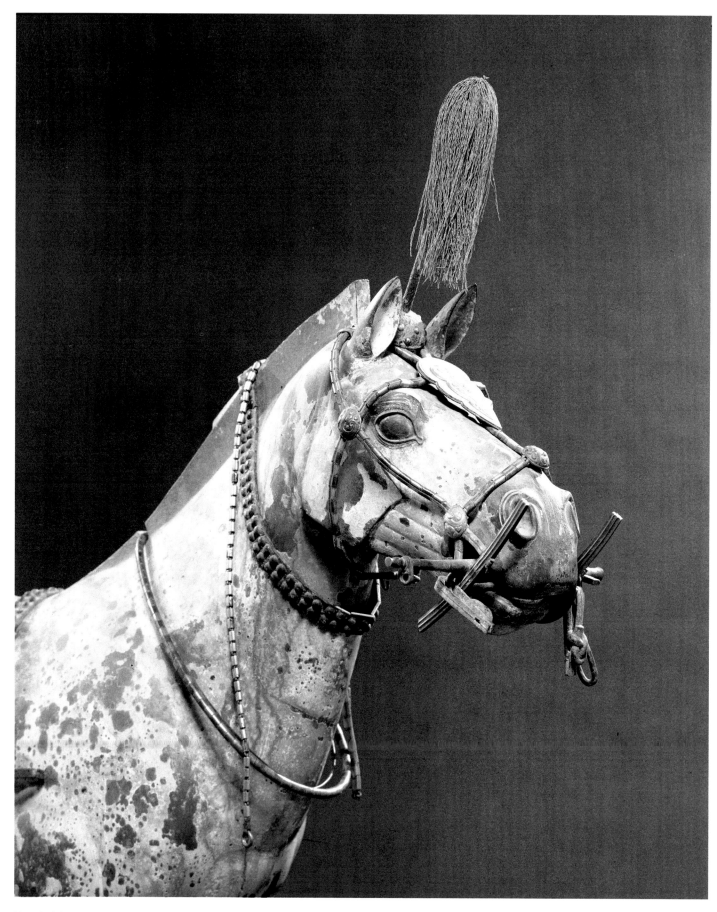

Head of the right side-horse with coarse-fiber tassel

Color-painting: Both chariots were originally painted with bright colors ranging from vermilion, pink, green, blue to white, but the basic color was white. Chinese ancestors believed "Ying-Yang" theory. According to this theory, the space and the earth were divided into five directions, which were represented by five colors- red, black, yellow, blue and white, representing the south, the north, the center, the east and the west respectively. So this set of bronze chariots and horses used basic white color to indicate the west direction. It can also foretell that the other four-colored bronze chariots and horses probably will be discovered in future around the emperor's tomb. This is the most important and most outstanding characteristic of the bronze chariots and horses.

More than ten kinds of color patterns were depicted on the chariots, most of which were dragons, phoenixes, diamonds, clouds and geometric designs. The layer of color painting has protected the bronze, delayed the process of oxidation. This is what the Qin people could not realize at the time.

Color patterns on the inner side of the front board of No.1 Chariot

Color patterns on the cabin-walls of No.2 Chariot

6 The newly unearthed pit--Stone Armor and Helmets:

In 1998, some 200 meters southeast away from the emperor's tomb, archaeologists discovered a large burial pit containing stone armor and helmets. The pit is rectangular in shape, covering an area of 13,600 square meters. It is the largest burial pit that has been unearthed so far within the confines of the inner and outer walls. Recent excavations unearthed nearly 120 stone armor suits and 90 stone helmets and some other relics. These objects were scattered in disarray on the bottom of the pit when discovered. Inside the pit, several pillars supported a wooden ceiling, which were coated by layers of straw. Different sections of the pit were separated by rammed earth.

View of excavation site of the pit of the stone armor and helmets

The armor and helmet were made from numerous stone flakes. The stone material was fine-grained limestone in a dark gray color. The stone they made from is easy to break, with poor toughness and heavy weight. The main flakes are rectangular, square, trapezoid and round in shape, some are in special shape. There are some round and square tiny holes on the stone flakes for stringing with flat copper wires. The edge of non-overlapped flakes is artistically decorated by a groove. The overlapped corners are made round with the aim of linking, expanding and contracting flakes. Judging from the features, archaeologists divide the armor suits into three categories:

Small stone flakes: Two pieces of this kind armor have been unearthed. The stone pieces are small and thin but exquisitely made, just like fish scales. Both armor suits are composed of over 800 stone flakes.

Medium stone flakes: This kind takes up over 80% of the stone armors that have been discovered. Most of the stone flakes are in rectangular or square shape with tiny holes for linking or for decoration.

Large stone flakes: Only one piece of this kind has been unearthed. It is 1.8 meters in length with armor flakes measuring 14 cm.by 7 cm. From its shape and structure, it's believed to be used for the battle steed. Historical book tells that the horse armor didn't appear until the end of the Eastern Han Dynasty, but this armor pushed the origin of horse-armor-making at least 400 years earlier.

At the present time, only one set of stone armor and one stone helmet have been restored. The armor weighs about 18 kilograms and the helmet weighs about 3.1 kilograms with 74 flakes linked together.

The objects were made the same size as real armor coats and helmets. According to archaeologists, they were not for practical use like the iron or leather armor of that era. These might have been specially made as funeral objects for Emperor QinShihuang .

To restore the stone armor

The restored stone armor suit

The restored stone helmet

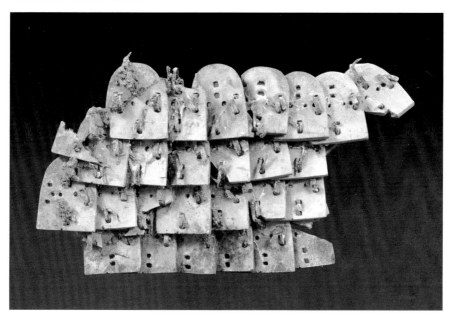

Restored piece of the stone armor suit

7 The newly unearthed pit--Terra-cotta Acrobats and a Bronze Tripod:

In addition to the chamber of armor, archaeologists have found another pit 40 meters south of the stone armor and helmet pit. The trial excavation on an area of only 9 square meters of the pit in rectangular shape unearthed 12 pottery figurines and "No.1 Bronze Tripod" of the Qin Dynasty on the top layer of the same pit.

Similar to real people in size, the figures were only clothed in a short skirt in a shape similar to those of woman's miniskirt today. Some appear tall and strong while some others short and slim. Exquisitely made, the figures vary in posture. One has his hand raised and another holds a piece of his skirt. Compared with the serious expressions on the Terra-cotta Warriors, these figures were more active and expressive.

According to an analysis of the restored figures, archaeologists said, different from the Terra-cotta Warriors, these pottery figures might be the acrobats who served in the Emperor Qin's imperial palace, portraying the splendid acrobatic art of the Qin Dynasty.

The restored pottery acrobats

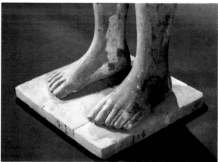

The restored pottery acrobats

The bronze Tripod unearthed on the top of the 12 acrobats is the biggest and heaviest one which has been found so far from the Emperor Qin's Mausoleum. It is 59.5 centimeters in length, 64 centimeters in diameter and 212 kilograms weigh.

The Tripod was originally a cooking utensil for boiling meat. With the consolidation of the system of hierarchical rites and music, Ding also became a symbol of stratum. This bronze tripod was delicately shaped with rich, fluid and beautiful patterns. Again, due to the lack of historical records, experts estimated that it might be a piece of sacrificial offering of that era.

The bronze Tripod unearthed on the top layer of the acrobats

One leg of the bronze Tripod

The newly unearthed pottery
civil official

8 The newly unearthed pit--CivL Officials:

In October 2,000, another new burial pit located southwest of the Emperor's tomb mound was discovered.

Only a few pottery figures unearthed from the pit have been restored and two of them are on display in the Museum temporarily. Both figures have colorful paint remained on the faces. Their facial expression is gentle and humble. They dress in similar costume as the pottery warriors in the burial army pits located 1.5 kilometers east away. The hands have no weapons, but cross at the waist and covered by long, loose sleeves. Each of them wears a knife and a knife-sharpener at the waist. The knife was used as the present eraser for peeling wrong notes inscribed on wood or bamboo, because paper had not been invented during the Qin period. The unique knife and knife-sharpener are the first of their kind so far unearthed from the emperor's Mausoleum.

It is estimated that these pottery figures might be the low ranking civil officials who served in the Central Government of Qin Empire.

The construction of QinShihuang's Mausoleum required considerable resources and manpower at that time. In present day, continuous excavations are going on. Archaeologists are sure that more and more treasures will be brought to light in future.

Knife and knife-sharpener on the waist of the civil official

Head of the pottery civil official

5.

It was in March 1974, when local farmers were drilling a well in search of water, that large pottery fragments were discovered 1.5 kilometers east of Emperor Qin's Mausoleum. This finds subsequently led to the revelation of one pit of the First Emperor's buried army 2,200 years ago. Since then continual archaeological work on excavation discovered another two pits successively. It has been revealed that three underground pits totally cover an area of 22,000 square meters, housing an estimated 8,000 life-size pottery warriors and horses.

The three pits were built in similar basic construction. They are five to seven meters beneath the present ground level with the terra-cotta figures placed in corridors. The corridors, divided by earth-rammed partition walls, are paved with pottery bricks on which the figures were placed. The earth walls sustained wood roof that was composed of huge and strong rafters, the roof was covered by layers of fiber mats, earth fill and tilled earth. All these were constructed to totally conceal the army.

The three pits vary in size and shape. Pit 1 is the largest one in rectangular shape, housing the main force of the army; Pit 2 is located some 20 meters north of Pit 1, which is a complex battle formation formed by charioteers, archers, cavalrymen and infantrymen. It is specially used for supporting the main force; Pit 3, located 25 meters to the north of Pit 1 and to the west of Pit 2, was evidently the headquarters. The total three pits are located to the east of Emperor's Mausoleum, determining that the army was facing east, with its back to the tomb, serving as guardians to protect the entrance of the Emperor's burial.

The first discovery of the terracotta Pit 1 in 1974

Pit 1:

Pit 1, the largest pit, is in a rectangular shape. It measures 230 meters long from east to west, 62 meters wide from north to south and 5 meters deep, covering an area of 14,260 square meters. Five sloping roadways into the pits were constructed on eastern and western sides of pits to permit access.

The terra-cotta warriors and horses are arrayed in a practical battle formation. At the eastern end of the pit there are three rows of vanguards, 68 in each, totaling 204 soldiers who were originally equipped with genuine bows and crossbows. Immediately behind the vanguards is the main body of the battle formation: 30 chariots, each of which was drawn by four horses, armored and unarmored soldiers held weapons originally, such as spears, halberds etc. Around the outer edge, there is one row of soldiers with crossbows facing south, north and west respectively as the flanks to guard the sides and rear of the army. According to the density of each trial trench that has been excavated, it's assumed that more than 6,000 pottery warriors and horses will be unearthed from Pit 1, most of which are infantrymen.

General view of Pit 1 with restored figures replaced in their original position. Excavation work is still continuing

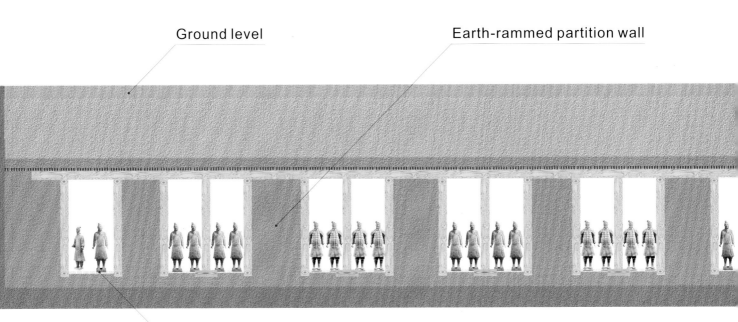

Ground level

Earth-rammed partition wall

Bricks

Drawing of a cross-section of Pit 1 showing the timber framework that was constructed over the corridors housing the terra-cotta figures

N

◻ Sloping roadway ═⋯⋯ Excavated and un-excavated earth-rammed partition wall ▢▤ Chariot drawn by four horses ○ Un-armored warrior ◖ Armored warrior

Diagram of Pit 1 showing the estimated layout of the 6,000 pottery figures and horses

Layers of timber, fiber matting, earth fill and tilled earth

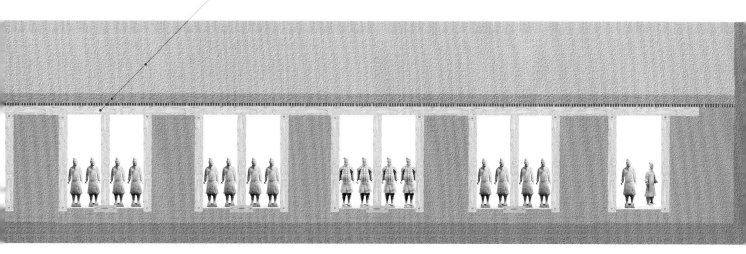

0   2m

Side view of Pit 1

Awakened
Qin's Terra-Cotta Army

Section of the battle array in Pit 1

The remnants of a chariot wheel in Pit 1

Side view of vanguards in Pit 1

Pit 2:

Located 20 meters to the north of Pit 1 at the eastern end, Pit 2 is in "L" shape with a protruding rectangular area at the northeast corner. This pit was discovered in 1976, covering an area of 6,000 square meters. Different from Pit 1, over 1,300 pottery figures in Pit 2 were placed in four specialized military forces:

The protruding northeast area houses 332 archers in all, 160 kneeling archers were arrayed into four columns with 172 standing archers surrounding. All these archers, whatever kneeling or standing soldiers, face eastward.

The south area is composed of war chariots. Total 64 chariots were arrayed in 8 columns, also facing east, eight chariots with their chariot horses in each column. Originally made of wood, the chariots were completely deteriorated when unearthed. Each chariot in this group was accompanied with a charioteer, who was flanked by two attendant soldiers carrying long weapons.

The middle area consists of war chariots in the front, immediately followed by infantrymen and the cavalry at the rear.

The north area has only cavalry. There are totally 108 cavalrymen. Each of the cavalrymen stands in front of his saddled war-horse, holding the reins in right hand and a bow in left hand.

The four arrays seemed to exist independently, but could be assembled immediately to constitute a complete battle formation during the war times. This reflected the unique military strategy of the Qin army - army array within army array.

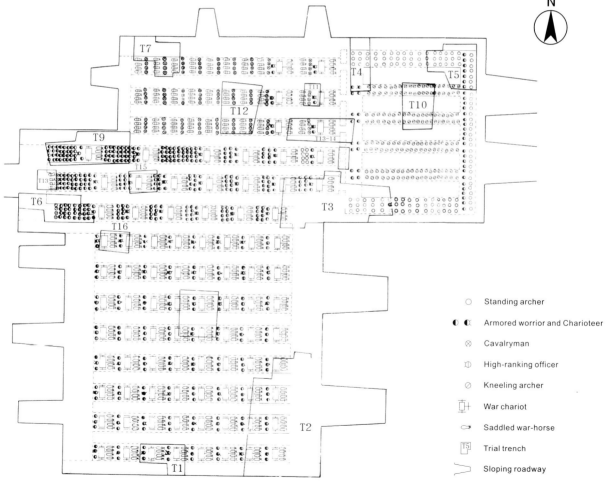

Diagram of Pit No.2 showing layout of pottery figures and chariots

Excavated site of Pit 2

Excavated site of the chariots in Pit 2

Excavated site of the kneeling archers in Pit 2

The remnants of wood used to support the roof in Pit 2

Pit 3 :

It is the smallest of the three pits and was discovered in 1976. Only 68 pottery figures and one chariot drawn by four horses were unearthed in the pit. It is of U-shape about 520 square meters. Pit 3 is now known as the command center of the entire army, because the following reasons:

Its position in the far northwest corner of the overall plan ensured that it was well protected by the armies of the two larger pits.

At the eastern end of the pit, there is a sloping road served as the entrance, then followed by an ornate canopied chariot with four armored officers. The chariot with canopy was colorful painted, representing higher rank.

In the north and south side chambers, 64 fully armored figures were found. Unlike the soldiers in Pit 1 and Pit 2, these figures were arrayed face-to- face with their backs to the wall, suggest that they were the guards. Even the weapons held by these guards are different from those in another two pits. One particular weapon named "Shu", which had no blades, only unearthed from Pit 3, it was believed to be used by the guards of honor.

In the north chamber, a piece of broken deer horn and some remains of animal bones were found at one time. They were used by generals as ritual objects for those religious practices, praying for the protection from the Gods before each battle.

Once the terra-cotta warriors and horses were all arrayed inside the corridors, the entrances were closed. It meant a sealed united army was formed to guard Emperor Qin's underground palace.

北廂房

車馬房
STABLE

鹿角遺跡
THE HISTORICAL REMAINS
OF THE WEAPONS

戰車遺跡
THE HISTORICAL REMAINS
OF THE WAR CHARIOT

General view of Pit 3

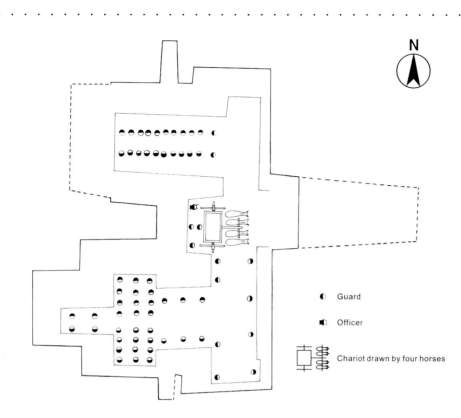

N

◐ Guard

◼ Officer

Chariot drawn by four horses

Diagram of Pit 3 showing layout of pottery figures and the single chariot of the commander

Restored chariot section of Pit 3

Restored south section of Pit 3

Restored pottery figures in the south section of Pit 3

Excavated north site of Pit 3

Awakened
Qin's Terra-Cotta Army

6.

In China the pottery figures could be dated back long time ago. But the pottery figures before the Qin Dynasty (221 BC-206 BC) were roughly made in small size and the temperature for baking in the kiln was low, too. The Qin Terra-cotta Warriors and Horses were big in life-size and exquisitely made with high technology. The hardness of their bodies indicates that they might be fired at a temperature between 950 and 1,050 degrees centigrade.

All of the soldiers and horses were made using local clay. The weight of the Terra-cotta Warriors varies from 110 kilos to 300 kilos. Their average height is 1.8 meters. How were these large and heavy statues made 2,200 years ago? Investigations into the construction of the figures have shown that the same method was used throughout the entire production. In general the bodies, heads and arms of the human figures are hollow and legs solid. The legs of the horses are also solid pottery, and these support a hollow body and head. Clearly such large figures could not have been produced from single mold and it seemed they were constructed from a number of separately molded or modeled segments that were glued together before firing.

The construction of the human figures required a number of steps. The clay was sifted and washed to ensure an even texture and color and was combined with ground quartz. After repeated kneading, the wet clay would achieve the right degree of firmness. The feet and the pedestal on which they stood were hand made or molded with the legs. The torso was either sculpted from strips of clay or cast prior to the attachment of the arms. All the joints would have been sealed and strengthened with clay coils. The final step was the creation of the head. The heads of the human figures were made in two-piece molds that were joined together later. Ears, noses and hair were hand made independently and then added on. In order to create an individualized appearance for each of the figures, such facial features as the mouth, moustache and beard and hairstyles were sculpted by probably a sharp bamboo. No two figures unearthed so far have the same features or expression. Some experts think that real soldiers served as models when Terra-cotta Warriors were made. Besides different faces, features as the armor

plates with fixings, belt hooks, shoe ties and costume details were precisely sculpted. After each statue was finished, the craftsmen were ordered to inscribe or print their names on the backs of robes, legs or armor. The names of over 80 craftsmen have been so far discovered. These seemed to be "2000-year-ago quality contro"l.

The same principles of construction were employed in the making of the horses. The legs of the horses are all solid pottery to ensure that they would be strong. The head, body and tail were all molded or modeled separately and then fixed to the legs. The various details of the eyes, nostrils and mouth of the horses were sculpted same as the human figures. Both the chariot and cavalry horses have a square cut mane, a neatly manicured two-pronged forelock and alert ears. The cavalry horse has a long, plaited and pendant tail and the chariot horse a shorter tied tail so as to keep it free of the harness and chariot shaft. The most visible difference between the types is the molded detail of the saddle and girth on the cavalry horse.

After the Terra-cotta Warriors and Horses were made, they were put into the kilns to be fire. The heads of the human figures were fired separately from the body, so the necks were left like holes. Both horse types have round holes in each side of the body, too. These holes could permit the gases and vapors that would have built up in the kiln to escape, prevent the figures from deforming or exploding.

Sketch Model Of The Construction Of The Pottery Human Figure

Sketch Model Of The Construction Of The Pottery Horse

One piece of the head molds with hand's trace left by craftsman 2,200 years ago

Strips of clay for coiling the torso of the pottery human figure

The individualized facial characteristics of the Terra-cotta Warriors

Hairstyles of the Terra-cotta Warriors

Belt buckles of the Terra-cotta Warriors

Beards and mustaches of the Terra-cotta Warriors

Shoes and shoe ties of the Terra-cotta Warriors

Inscriptions of the names of craftsmen on the Terra-cotta Warriors

The head of the pottery horse

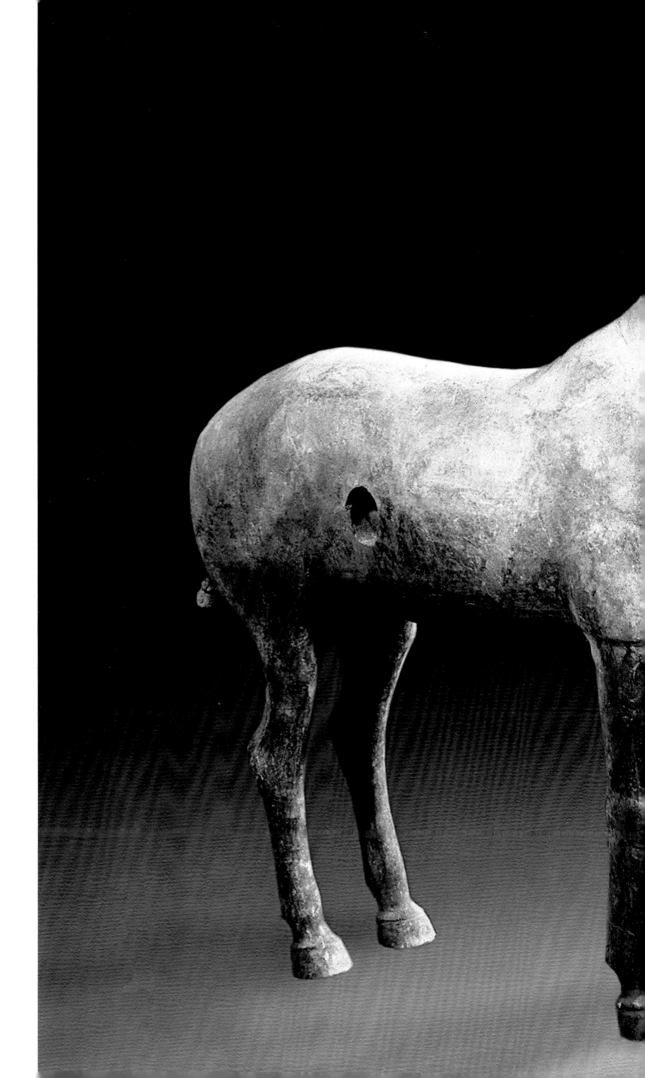

Full view of a chariot horse with holes for permitting the gases and vapors in the kiln to escape

The tied tail of the chariot horse

The plaited pendant tail of the cavalry horse

The saddle and girth on the cavalry horse

Awakened
Qin's Terra-Cotta Army

7.

The range of terra-cotta figure types represented in QinShihuang's army is more extensive. There are about seven main categories as follows: high-ranking officer, officer, armored and unarmored soldier, charioteer, cavalryman, kneeling archer and standing archer. The officer class is identified by their greater size and more ornate armor including headgear and small tabs or sashes which may be emblems of rank. The cavalryman is immediately identifiable by the tight fitting helmet tied under the chin, together with tight fitting armor to the waist and flared robe to facilitate riding. The charioteer is identifiable by the fully armored sleeves and the position of the hands, held firmly out in front as if to hold the reins.

Archaeologists have determined that originally the figures were completed with painted detail, but ravages of floods, fire and time have erased original paint from statues. However, guided by flakes of paint remained on the figures, an approximation of the figures' original appearances can be modified as follows. Two new points can be known from them: Qin army had no standardized colors for uniform and various colors can not help distinguish different ranks. It means that warriors of different ranks sometimes wore same color clothing homely made.

Paint fragments on the collar and armor

The remnants of paints of a pottery figure

99

High Ranking Officer, Possibly A General
Height 197 cm,
From Pit 2, Qin Terra-cotta Museum

The officer's gesture and size give him a majestic presence. He is wearing double-layered robes covered by shoulder plates. Evidence suggests that his outer robe were painted dark purple and the robe beneath vermilion. His trousers were in green and his square-toed shoes black. The headgear he is wearing was painted brown. The colorful fish-scaled armor protected the chest, back and shoulders. The armor was usually painted brown and dotted with vermilion thread for linking the pieces.

The collar, chest, shoulders and edges of the armor were decorated with colorful patterns. There are eight knots made of ribbon to decorate the armor, three knots on the front plate, three on the back and one knot each on the shoulder. His carefully groomed mustache and sideburns convey a sense of authority, solemnity and dignity.

High ranking officer

Painted reconstruction of high ranking officer

Officer

From Pit 2, Qin Terra-cotta Museum

. . . .

The officer was wearing red trousers and a high-collar robe in green under an armor cape originally. The collar and cuff were decorated by white and red patterns. Both his flat hat and square-toed shoes should be in black color. The figure wears chest armor, which is fastened by cross-straps on the back, over a flared battle robe. The ornate scarves around the neck possibly signify his commissioned rank.

From the position of the hands and arms, it's clear that this figure held weapons.

Front view of the officer

Rear view of the officer

Painted reconstruction of officer

The Armored and Un-armored Soldiers: A large quantity of soldiers has been discovered from the terra-cotta pits. Some of them wear armor, some don't. The colors of their uniform were much different when they painted. But the armors were all painted brown, without the colorful patterns on. The robes varied in colors as vermilion, green or blue, and the trousers green, white or pink.

Un-armored Soldier
From Pit 1 Qin Terra-cotta Museum
· ·
The figure wears knee-length robe without armor-plated uniform. Around the waist of the robe is a belt linked with a distinctive belt hook. The soldier also wears the short trousers and his shoes curve upward. The hair is tightly coiled into a neat bun on the right top of his head. The fact that he wears no armor allows for unrestricted movement.

Armored Officer.
Height 182 cm,
From Pit 3 Qin Terra-cotta Museum
· ·
The figure wears a battle robe with full body armor including shoulder pieces. He also wears short trousers, curve-toed shoes. The right arm is raised and would evidently have held spear.

Un-armored soldier

Armored officer

Charioteer With His Attendant Soldiers

From Pit 2 Qin Terra-cotta Museum

The figure was provided with a special uniform with extra armor to protect his arms, hands, neck and upper body. This was necessary because he needed to use both hands to hold the reins, and thus could not defend himself. His hands held firmly out in front to hold the reins.

The attendant soldiers, who flank the charioteer, wear long robes in different colors, one is in red, another in green. Both soldiers carry long weapons in one hand while grasping the chariot with the other.

Charioteer flanked by two soldiers

Painted reconstruction of the right and left flanking soldiers

Cavalryman With His Saddled War-Horse

From Pit 2 Qin Terra-cotta Museum

The cavalry was an important element of Emperor Qin's army, providing it with speed and agility. The figures of cavalrymen so far discovered were placed in Pit 2, together with their horses.

This figure wears the short dark brown tight-fitting armor, green narrow-sleeved knee-length robe originally. Beneath the belted waist the robe appears full with pleats and folds. The small tight-fitting cap fastened under the chin was originally painted a reddish brown, suggesting leather. The stitched leather shoes are represented in some detail with laces and ties. The figure holds the reins in one hand and a crossbow in the other.

The molded saddle on the horse's back with hand-finished carved probably represents a leather originally. A series of black circles symbolizing tacks are molded on the surface of the saddle, which were painted red, white, brown and blue. The saddle was held in place by a girth underneath the belly of horse.

Cavalryman with his horse

Kneeling Archer

Height, 120cm

From Pit 2 Qin Terra-cotta Museum

The figures of kneeling archers were discovered from Pit 2. They own quite similar characteristics.

The figure wears green battle robe covered by armor together with shoulder pieces. The battle robe was distinguished by the series of pleats and folds as it rests over the legs. As with all of the terra-cotta figures, the archer was highly detailed, even showing the pebbled surface texture on the soles of his shoes. The hair was plaited on the back of the head and then coiled into a bun tied with vermilion ribbons.

He kneels on the right knee with the left knee raised. The right arm is held with the hand open, the left arm rests on the raised left knee and the hand extends across the chest. The pose of both hands evidences that this figure held one crossbow originally. The head is held firm and the eyes look directly ahead. The straight back emphasizes the impressions of concentration and discipline.

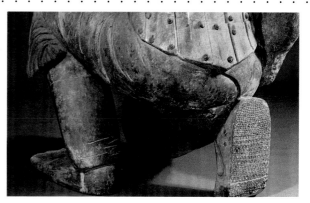

Rear view of part of the kneeling archer

Sole of archer's shoes

Painted reconstruction of the kneeling archer

Kneeling archer

Standing Archer
· · · · · · · · · · · · · ·
Height, 178 cm

From Pit 2 Qin Terra-cotta
Museum

There is a large number of standing archers discovered in Pit 2. Their uniforms were colorful painted when made.

This figure was dressed in an unarmored red robe fastened around the waist with a belt, short green trousers, white shin guards and short boots. His hair was coiled into a neat bun on the right top of his head. The archer displays a posture: the feet stand apart with the right foot turned outwards and the left foot forward. His body is carefully tilted to the left with his pendant left arm and raised right arm in front of the chest as if to hold a crossbow.

Standing archer

8.

The Terra-cotta Army is not only a huge subterranean military battle formation, but also an armory of the Qin Dynasty. Approximately tens of thousands of weapons have been unearthed from the partly excavated section of the pits. The weapons can be divided into three categories: long weapons, short weapons and long range weapons, such as spear, halberd, Shu, Pi, sword, Wu hook and cross-bow etc. Especially Pi and Wu hook are the first of their kind so far unearthed.

In ancient Chinese records there is much about Pi Weapon, but no complete weapon has ever been unearthed. Pi weapon belongs to long weapons. Its head is about 30 cm long and looks like a dagger. A 3-meter long shaft is attached to its head. Pi is such kind of sharp weapons used to bayonet.

Bronze Pi weapon

Wu hook belongs to short weapons. It looks like a crescent moon and there are blades on both edges. Its head is flat and easy to hook. It first appeared in the State of "Wu", hence the name "Wu hook".

Some 30 bronze Shu weapons were unearthed in Pit 3. Shu weapon in Qin Dynasty was used for ceremonial purposes and a symbol of authority. It is shaped in a cylinder with the head looks like a triangular cone. The warriors in the Pit 3 with holding Shu weapons strengthened majestic atmosphere of the headquarters.

Bronze Shu weapon

Wu hook

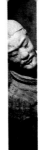

Swords had the highest rank among the weapons in ancient China and were carried by well-known or high-ranking people. About 17 swords have been discovered so far from the Terra-cotta pits. Besides the general, some officers have swords in their hands, too. The longest sword is about 94.4cm, and the shortest one is 81cm. The sword discovered intact from Pit 1 originally would have been kept in a wooden scabbard that has been rotted. Its blade is narrow and thin with a ridge along the center. According to analysis, the surface of the sword contains 0.6 to 2% chromium, with a thickness of 10 micron, which acted as a protective coating against corrosion during the long burial. The modern chrome-plating technology appeared in western countries in 1920s to 1930s, but it had emerged in China 2,200 years before. In style and appearance the sword resembles the classic Zhou sword which continued to be used in the succeeding Han Dynasty.

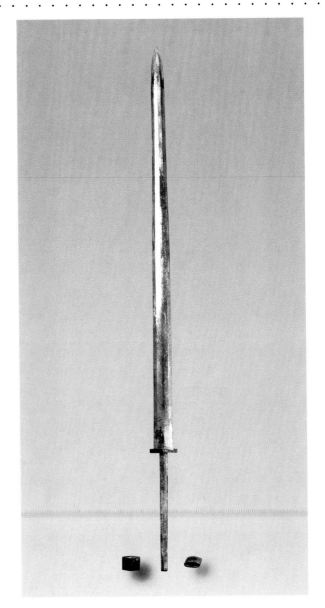

Bronze sword

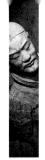

Archaeologists have found almost every kind of weapons the Qin soldiers once used from the pits. The Qin weapons are not only in wide coverage, large number, but also advanced in technology. Ancient craftsmen had consciously regulated the proportions of the three main ingredients of bronze: copper, tin and lead, for casting weapons in different kinds. The bronze swords have a higher percentage of tin (21.3%) than in other bronze pieces from the excavation. This higher tin content resulted in an increased hardness comparable with tempered carbon steel. Advanced anti-rust technology of metal is another magnificent character of the Qin bronze weapons. Although the bronze swords had been buried for more than 2,000 years, they looked as shiny as new when they were unearthed, and could cut 19 layers of paper. It was the chrome-plating technology 2,000 years ago protected the sharpness of the swords.

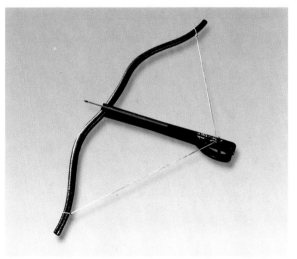

Crossbow

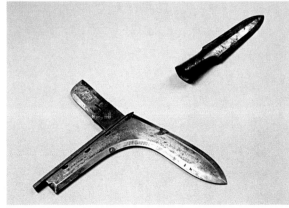

Bronze halberd

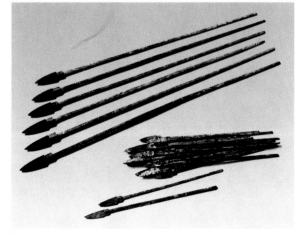

Bronze arrows

Crossbows and arrowheads belong to long range weapons. The trigger mechanism for a crossbow is a type that, having been invented towards the end of the Zhou Dynasty, quickly found favor and was widely used in Qin Dynasty. The trigger is composed of four separately cast pieces and is very much more powerful than any of its contemporary weapons as it could, fire a bronze arrowhead a distance of 800 meters. The arrowheads, the largest number among the weapons unearthed, are extremely sharp.

The unearthed weapons demonstrate that Chinese metallurgy reached a high level in the Qin Dynasty. The Qin weapons were even standardized made then. Analysis has shown that the pointed heads of the arrows are triangular cones with equal sides. The two bolts on all the crossbow triggers are interchangeable. The arms manufacturing industry was well developed and strictly administered by the Qin State, too. A number of excavated weapons from the terra-cotta pits have brief inscription, describing the name of official unit for manufacturing arms. We can believe that the most advanced technology and top craftsmen of that era were involved in creating these brilliant bronze weapons.

Crossbow trigger

Bronze dagger with inscription

Bronze spear with inscription

9.

According to ShiJi (Records of Historians), XiangYu, a rebel in the Qin Dynasty, burnt Emperor Qin's palace and his mausoleum in 206 BC. So the construction of the pits was damaged during the fire. The collapsed roof pressed the Terra-cotta Warriors and Horses into fragments. None of them was completed when unearthed. Mending broken figures becomes a painstaking work for archaeological workers.

There is a company of partly assembled statues at the western end of Pit 1, where located the temporary restoration site of the museum now. Buried beneath them, more Terra-cotta Warriors and Horses await to be unearthed. A group of skilled workers toil here everyday to test the missing parts and try to make the right connections. Thousands of fragments awaiting connection have lain for years in long piles on the ground. Some fragments have marks on to indicate where the item was found and to which statue it might belong, but most don't. According to the marks, the pieces were glued together by epoxy resin. Most of time, each statue would take a

few months to be mended. If the workers can find one piece that fits in a day, that will be a lucky day. The final restoration step is to patch up the statues and then they will be sent back to the original places where they were found.

Every since the Terra-cotta Warriors and Horses were discovered 25 years ago, the flaking off of the paint has tormented archaeological experts from around the world. After years of research, two new technological methods were invented by a team of experts of the Terra-cotta Museum and further developed in co-operation with experts from the Cultural Relics Office of Bavaria of Germany since 1996. These two inventions are known as PEG200 and HEMA and now extensively applied on the newly unearthed kneeling archers from Pit 2. They can keep the original paint on the statues from fading and flaking after being brought to light.

Archaeological experts revealed that craftsmen in the Qin Dynasty first painted a layer of lacquer on the surface of the sculptured warriors, and then colored them with paint made of minerals. The water remained in the layer of lacquer evaporated

soon after the warriors being unearthed and made the paint layer get creased.

The aim of two inventions is to replace the water in the lacquer layer and keep the paint on the lacquer layer from getting creased. The experts of the museum covered the colored Terra-cotta Warriors with a solvent of PEG200, which slowly permeates into the lacquer layer to replace the water.

The other way is using a special chemical, dubbed HEMA, before stabilizing the paint by electronic beaming.

Both inventions worked, but the HEMA is now used more often than the PEG200 because experiments have revealed that it works better on large pieces than the PEG200.

Unearthed fragments of the pottery figures

Excavated site of Pit 1

A heap of unearthed heads of the pottery warriors

The temporary restoration site, located at the western end of Pit 1

Unearthed fragments of the pottery horses

The restoration of a pottery figure

Excavated site of the colorful kneeling archers in Pit 2

Unearthed pottery head with a green face

The flaking off of the paint on the face of the pottery figure

Preservation at the excavated site

Awakened
Qin's Terra-Cotta Army

Editors-in-chief ◆ Meng Jianmin   Zhang Lin

Executive editor ◆ Dai Xiaonuo

Writer ◆ Zhang Lin

Photographer ◆ Xia Juxian   Guo yan

Designer ◆ Dragon-Mountain Culture Spread Co.,Ltd.

Executive Printer ◆ Liu Qinghai

Publisher ◆ Shaanxi Travel & Tourism Press

Printed by Printing House of Xi'an Conservatory of Music

ISBN7-5418-1820-8/K·151

First Print，October 2001